Human Rights: Rhetoric or Reality

EDITORS

George W. Forell

William H. Lazareth

JUSTICE

BOOKS

FORTRESS PRESS   PHILADELPHIA

Library of Congress Cataloging in Publication Data

Main entry under title:

Human rights : rhetoric or reality.

(Justice books)
Bibliography: p.
1.   Civil rights—Moral and religious aspects.
I.   Forell, George Wolfgang, 1919-   II.   Lazareth,
William Henry, 1928-   III.   Series.
JC571.H778   261.7   77-20537
ISBN 0-8006-1553-0

6515C78   Printed in the United States of America   1–1553

Contents

Human Rights: Rhetoric or Reality

George H. Brand*

IN the realm of politics, ideas have a way of coming back to haunt us. This seems to be especially true in the formulation of both domestic and foreign policy. A policy is a course of action initiated by political leaders for the purpose of influencing decisions and determining events. It serves as a guiding principle in the attempt to promote a social order that is consistent with the sociopolitical values of a particular state.

Yet political history reveals that the human intellect has never been able fully to anticipate or to control the consequences of even the most carefully designed policy. Once a policy is set in motion it becomes an independent force with a capacity to provoke actions that were unforeseen and unintended. Confining the effects of a particular policy to a specifically prescribed set of objectives has strained the ability of even the most artful statesmanship. Ideas, once unleashed, have a dynamic of their own, and can challenge the very foundations from which they arose.

Both the American and Soviet experience with the human rights issue bears this out. The ideological consequences of de-Stalinization, the political implications of the Final Act of the Conference on Security and Cooperation in Europe (CSCE)[1] and the global ramifications of President Carter's early stance on

---

*The author has taught political science and international affairs at Manhattanville and Barnard Colleges.
1. On August 1, 1975, in Helsinki, Finland, leaders of the thirty-five nations participating in the European Conference on Security and Cooperation, including all the nations of Europe (except Albania) plus the United States and Canada, signed a 100-page declaration on European Security.

human rights are cases in point. Each of these instances unleashed social and political forces that were not anticipated.

In other words, one is dealing here with a paradoxical situation, wherein a political leadership is engaged, at one and the same time, in a concerted attempt to *minimize* the effects of a particular policy on areas beyond the desired objective, and to *maximize* the usefulness of this policy in attaining the clearly defined benefits of that objective.

Listening to the official trumpets heralding human rights, it would seem helpful to analyze this process in the context of several distinct phases in the interaction between the Soviet Union, Eastern Europe, and the United States. These phases, while to some extent anchored in specific time periods, are not intended to represent precise chronological units. Periodization can only be a rough approximation of actual historical stages. The following discussion focuses on the main issues at stake rather than on chronologically precise historical accounts.

THE SOVIET DILEMMA: A CRISIS OF AUTHORITY

Khrushchev's dramatic repudiation of Stalinism at the Twentieth Party Congress in 1956 opened a Pandora's box, the contents of which continue to haunt the Soviet leadership. The "secret speech," as it was called, had a two-fold purpose: one domestic, the other, international.

On the domestic side, at a critical point in the succession struggle, Khrushchev found it expedient to become Stalin's accuser. Denouncing Stalin's arbitrary rule for its lawlessness, cruelty, and failure to respect party statutes, Khrushchev was able to persuade his colleagues and the rank and file members of the party that the previous system of institutionalized mass terror had come to an end.

The party bureaucracy was given a double pledge: (a) the secret police would not be used against them; (b) they would be consulted on all policy decisions according to statutory rules. Assuming the role of the destroyer of the Stalinist myth, Khrushchev associated himself with Lenin, subordinated the secret police to the party, and established a legitimate basis for his claim to rule by emerging as the reformer of the Soviet political system.

Thus committing himself to the party's supremacy, Khrushchev became increasingly dependent on the support of the party apparatus. Throughout his years as Premier, Khrushchev was unable to extricate himself from this self-imposed restriction. It seems somewhat ironic that the very changes that Khrushchev initiated in the social and political dynamics of the Soviet system eventually culminated in his own downfall. Yet, in retrospect, creating the conditions that led to his removal from office may well have been Khrushchev's major contribution to the social and political evolution of Soviet society.

Nonetheless, from an ideological perspective, Khrushchev's removal revealed a dismal picture of the ongoing quality of Soviet leadership. According to official Soviet history thus far, for almost twenty years Russian power was in the hands of a "paranoic mass murderer," and for almost ten years (1955–1964) power was in the hands of a "harebrained schemer."[2] What generous epithet is due Brezhnev after his departure is yet to be seen. At any rate, under such circumstances the Soviet concept of legitimate authority remains, at best, elusive. This lesson has not been lost on the East-European leadership as they increasingly question the validity of Moscow's claim to be the guiding party and the ruling center of the Communist movement.

On the international side, Khrushchev challenged the Stalinist notion that totalitarian rule and the socialist transformation of society could only be maintained by continuous revolutions from above through the ruthless exercise of state power. Departing from this previous policy, Khrushchev recognized the formal "equality" of sovereign Communist states. This de-Stalinization policy was intended to provide the basis for an ideological regeneration of international Communism, and thereby place the political leadership of the Soviet Union on a more solid foundation.

Rather than providing international Communism with a new

2. Bertram D. Wolfe, *Khrushchev and Stalin's Ghost* and *Problems in Communism*, July/August, 1965, U.S. Printing Office, Washington, D.C.

philosophical unity, Khrushchev's policy created such a severe political and ideological crisis in Eastern Europe that the Soviet bloc shook to its very core. Having come to power as the bearer of a new international order for the Communist world, Khrushchev was forced, albeit unwittingly, to preside over the systematic fragmentation of the Soviet Empire.

The Polish resistance and Hungarian uprising of 1956, the Sino-Soviet split, the intensified intellectual productivity of East-European Marxist revisionists attempting to restructure socialist society along humanistic lines, the Czechoslovakian Spring of 1968, Charter 77, the emergence of Eurocommunism in Western Europe, and the rise of the dissident movement within the Soviet Union itself, are all the offspring of de-Stalinization.

The ferment in Eastern Europe brought to the surface a moral revolution. In his brilliant essay "Responsibility and History" (1957), the Polish Marxist philosopher Leszek Kolakowski decried every form of arbitrary rule, rejected all absolutist ideologies as the inherent enemy of the spirit of free inquiry, and returned to a Kantian ethic by arguing that every individual must be treated as an end, never as a means. Rejecting the notion that at times the innocent must suffer for the sake of the revolution, Kolakowski insisted that it was never justified to demand that the present generation be sacrificed for the abstract vision of some distant utopia.

From Kolakowski and Schaff in Poland, to Markovic, Supek, and Vranicki in Yugoslavia, from Heller in Hungary to Kosik and Prucha in Czechoslovakia, there emerged in Socratic fashion a common search for new approaches to fundamental ethical questions.

The issue of human rights in East Europe focused on the relationship between socialism and democracy. Philosophical discussions concerning "the new model of socialism" were especially provocative in Czechoslovakia. The revisionist program called for government under law, demanded free expression of opinion in the religious sphere as well as in politics, and supported other basic rights associated with parliamentary democracy.

The common theme that permeated all the writings of the Marxist revisionists was the precedence of the individual over the social group. Particular invectives were levelled against elitism, and the Leninist theory of an elite party was singled out for special criticism. A political system based on the equality of free individuals and universal justice was the only one considered to be consistent with an industrial society. Viewing mass consumption as a social evil, the revisionists held that the individual in socialist society must first of all ponder the spiritual basis of existence. At a meeting of the Paulus Society in April, 1967, Marxist Milan Prucha went so far as to suggest that Christians show "greater radicalism in their striving for transcendent goals."[3]

In a speech at the Fourth Congress of the Czechoslovak Writers' Union, Ludvik Vaculik said:

> Freedom exists only where people do not need to speak of it. The party functionaries wish people wouldn't complain about what they see, but instead of changing what people see they are trying to change people's eyes. In the meantime we are losing the only ideal that is truly valuable: the dream of a government identical with the citizen, of a citizen who governs himself. Is this dream realizable?[4]

And in a statement of principle the philosopher Ivan Svitak asserted:

> Dictatorship must be replaced by an open society, the monopoly of power must be liquidated and the power elite be regulated by a free press. The bureaucratic control of society must give way before a just implementation of fundamental human rights . . .[5]

The courageous efforts of East-European intellectuals to construct a humane and moral socialist society established invaluable precedents and guidelines in the continuing struggle for human rights.

Little did Khrushchev suspect that the policy which he designed to provide a new ideological unity in Eastern Europe would instead unleash the forces of social and political pluralism, and culminate in an open challenge to the very foundations of Leninism.

3. Milan Prucha, ("To Be a Human Person: The Social Engagement of Philosophy"), in *Ost-Probleme* (Bonn), July, 1967, p. 429.
4. Ludvik Vaculik. From speech to the Fourth Congress of the Czechoslovak Writers' Union in Prague, published in *East Europe*, October, 1969.
5. Ibid.

HELSINKI AND BEYOND

Since the end of World War II, the Soviet Union has pursued two major objectives in its relations with Western Europe. The first objective was to obtain formal recognition by the West of the present borders in Europe, thereby guaranteeing the territorial status quo in East-Central Europe.

Since, in Soviet eyes, the military security of the USSR can only be protected by strict military control of East Europe, the second major objective was to obtain Western legitimization of Soviet supremacy in Eastern Europe. The Soviet Union has always given the highest priority to maintaining its vanguard position in the socialist community. Any sudden eruption or substantive political change as in Czechoslovakia is viewed as an unacceptable threat to that leadership role.

From the Soviet perspective, the consolidation of these policy objectives required a conference on European security and cooperation. Brezhnev stated the purposes of such a conference in his report to the Twenty-third Congress of the CPSU[6] in March of 1966:

"To discuss the existing proposals of the socialist and other states of Europe concerning a military detente and the reduction of armaments in Europe and the development of peaceful, mutually advantageous ties among all European states . . . To continue to seek ways for solving one of the cardinal tasks of European security—the peaceful settlement of the German question with a view to eliminating completely the vestiges of World War II in Europe *on the basis of recognition of the now existing European frontiers, including those of the two German states.*" [7]

Viewed politically, the Conference on Security and Cooperation in Europe (CSCE) at Helsinki represented many years of Soviet diplomatic efforts to gain formal recognition of the post-World War II situation in Europe through the confirmation of the status quo, including the division of Germany and recognition of Eastern Europe as an exclusive Soviet sphere of influence.

Soviet concessions to Western proposals on human rights were the necessary price for these political gains. The thirty-five signatories of the Final Act at Helsinki agreed—

6. Communist Party of the Soviet Union.
7. *Pravda,* March 30, 1966. Translated in *Current Digest of the Soviet Press,* April 13, 1966, p. 13.

". . . to respect human rights and fundamental freedoms, including the freedom of thought, conscience, religion or belief for all without distinction as to race, sex, language, or religion;" and, "to promote and encourage the effective exercise of civil, political, economic, social, cultural, and other rights and freedoms, all of which derive from the inherent dignity of the human person and are essential for his free and full development."[8]

As one might have anticipated, an intense debate concerning the interpretation of the Final Act quickly surfaced. While the United States maintained that all the principles of the Act are of equal importance and should be observed because they stand independently of each other, the Soviets argued that the Act must be read as a whole, and that the Act principle of nonintervention limits the operation of the provision dealing with human rights. The principle of human rights, according to the Soviet view, had to be interpreted in the context of all the other principles, including respect for the rights inherent in sovereignty and nonintervention in internal affairs.

The section on sovereign equality states that the signatories "will also respect each other's right freely to choose and develop its political, social, economic, and cultural systems as well as its right to determine its laws and regulations." And the section on nonintervention in internal affairs begins with the statement that the participating states "will refrain from any intervention, direct or indirect, individual or collective, in the internal or external affairs falling within the domestic jurisdiction of another participating State, regardless of their mutual relations."

This motivated one Soviet observer to write:

"In view of these clear statements, how is one to take the attempts by certain Western leaders to patronize people who come out against the socialist system which the Soviet people have established in their own country? Only as intervention in the internal affairs of the Soviet Union and disrespect for the Final Act and its priniciples."[9]

Petrov's statement is particulary ironic when one recalls that at an early session of the Security Conference a correspondent asked

8. Department of State Bulletin Reprint, *Conference on Security and Cooperation in Europe: Final Act*, Helsinki, 1975, Article VII, p. 3.

9. A. Petrov, "And What Is the Final Act?", *Moscow News, Supplement*, March 26—April 2, 1977, p. 14.

the Soviet spokesman whether the Soviet draft provision concerning "nonintervention in internal affairs of the other states" would
prevent recurrence of the Soviet invasion of Czechoslovakia and
was told that: "Assistance was granted . . . on the request of the
Czech government. There was no interference in Czech internal
affairs and this should continue to be so in the future."[10]

BALANCING DETENTE AND HUMAN RIGHTS

Several factors seem to have motivated the Carter administration to launch its human rights campaign early in 1977. Having
assumed the Presidency during a period that was experiencing a
serious erosion of popular confidence in public institutions in
general, and the executive branch in particular, the new President sought to build a policy consensus by focusing on some of the
basic, shared values of the American political tradition.

Carter was fully aware that the critical choices ahead required
an administration of national unity that could inspire broad support. Reviving public support for the American political institutions became the first priority. The initial enthusiasm which
greeted the new policy attested to the President's keen political
sense.

In the realm of foreign affairs, however, the policy had a less
happy outcome. Recognizing that the ideological struggle is a
two-way street, the emphasis on human rights was meant to encourage the dissident movement in the Soviet Union, and exacer-
bate the conflict between Soviet designs and East-European interests by creating centrifugal forces on the part of East-
European states. It was hoped that popular pressure for human
rights in these countries would serve as an active force in loosen-
ing the ties of the East-European governments with the USSR. In
fact, repression of dissidents tended to increase, and emigration
became more difficult. In addition, the new American approach
caused bewilderment among our European allies and created the
fear that an emphasis on moralism might prevent the exercise of
rational policy.

The President's personal letter to Soviet dissident Sakharov and
a White House meeting with the exiled Vladimir Bukovsky

10. *New York Times,* July 5, 1973.

evoked a strong Soviet reaction. During the SALT talks in Moscow, Brezhnev informed Secretary Vance that the Soviets considered the human-rights campaign a departure from the principle of noninterference in internal affairs. He also insisted that a continuation of the campaign could hinder further progress in the detente relationship. Carter was eventually persuaded to weaken his original position.

In summary, we find that recent human-rights initiatives have been motivated by pragmatic political needs and have been laid aside when they proved inconsistent with other national goals. The Helsinki agreement provided the Soviets with important political gains, but there clearly is little intent on their part to abide by the human-rights sections of that accord. The Carter human-rights statement also seems to have been motivated in part by the need for domestic support and unity, and it, too, was largely abandoned when it threatened the detente relationship with the USSR. Perhaps the lesson to be learned is that we should not look to the major political powers for substantive initiatives in the area of human rights.

MORALITY AND POLITICS

There are those who argue on moral grounds that a democratic state engages in complicity with the repressive practices of the Soviet Union if diplomatic relations are maintained without requiring Soviet observance of human rights. But is there not an equal or even greater moral obligation to participate in negotiations that reduce the likelihood of nuclear war? Neither the primitive anti-Communism of the right nor the empty slogans of the left offer a guide to policy.

The complexities of human existence force us to recognize that all political actions fall short of justice. Yet we have no choice but to act politically. By shirking from action because it is tinged with evil, the purist, in satisfying the demands of a self-righteous ego, eliminates the possibility of discriminating among different evils. The utopian ideologue thus perpetuates an even greater evil.

In a most perceptive and humane memorandum, the late William C. Gausmann, a State Department official, suggested procedures that would help further the cause of human rights.

First, the failure of President Kennedy's "Alliance for Progress" in this hemisphere, as well as the tragic and disasterous Johnson-Nixon policy in Indo-China should teach us that the United States can neither be a universal model for the development of democratic governments, nor can it be the world's policeman.

Second, a meaningful policy of human rights cannot only be concerned with external problems. Western criticism of Soviet repression must also take into account those instances where human rights are violated within Western boundaries. Specifically, a U.S. Helsinki Committee could have pointed to the continuing denial of human rights to agricultural workers in this country while at the same time keeping the plight of such workers in the Communist world on the international agenda.

Third, any attempt by the West to encourage secessionist tendencies on the part of the Soviet republics, or to undermine the Soviet governmental system, would be counter-productive. Such a policy would only serve to intensify Soviet repressive measures.

Fourth, international nongovernmental bodies should play a far greater role in pointing to human-rights violations wherever they exist. Such criticisms could not be interpreted as specifically anti-Soviet as they would be directed to every place on the globe. In addition, not being the act of any one government, these criticisms would have far greater moral persuasion and keep the issue of human rights on the international agenda. It was Socrates who observed that: "He who would really fight for justice must do so as a private citizen, not as a political figure . . . "[11]

The future evolution of the Soviet system cannot be predicted. Whether, with the passing of Brezhnev, the new leadership emerges from a younger generation of technocrats whose commitment to economic modernization frees it from the shackles of a sterile ideology remains to be seen. If that were to happen, we might witness a gradual transformation of the present bureaucratic dictatorship into a more pluralistic system. Under the present circumstances, however, the cause of human rights would be better served by the slow evolutionary forces operating within both Soviet and East-European society.

11. Plato, *Apology*, The Library of Liberal Arts, p. 38.

Perhaps the most important and unexpected consequence of President Carter's initial policy is that it legitimized the concern for human-rights violations on the international agenda. It is at this point that nongovernmental agencies can make a lasting contribution by keeping that concern alive. Judiciously to be avoided, however, is a human-rights policy that declares: "Only Victims East of the Elbe Need Apply."

THE MOTE IN OUR OWN EYE

A meaningful doctrine of human rights recognizes every member of the species *Homo sapiens* as human and has as its primary goal the enhancement of human dignity. To have freedom of speech and assembly while living in squalor is as inimical to human dignity as is living in relative economic security while being denied fundamental rights of self-expression. Though we readily perceive the political injustices of the Soviet sphere, we show a peculiar blindness to the economic injustices of our own system. The commitment must be made to economic, as well as to political and civil rights.

But this will not be an easy task in the future that awaits us. As we approach the end of an era of easy expansion and slowly move into an era of a more cautious and monitored growth, we can anticipate dynamically mounting socio-economic crises. This awareness will create a framework in which discussions about social, political, and economic rights become all the more difficult.

Seventeenth-century Lockean liberalism has dominated Western political thought for the past 200 years. This liberalism has spent itself because it has become irrelevant. Its sacred premises of individualism, unbridled competition, and unlimited growth are no longer compatible with our social experience, and will have to yield to a new social and political philosophy.

Are we in the West willing to adjust economic priorities when it becomes evident that what is needed from the perspective of the entire community is not always in harmony with the expectations of the corporate producers? Will we, in other words, opt for a system of production that is geared to maximum social need rather than to maximum corporate profit? Or will we obstinately cling to the economic priorities and institutional arrangements of a by-gone era?

For instance, will we in the United States continue to pour billions of dollars into an interstate highways program at the cost of inadequate mass transit and increased pollution? Is this serving the public good, or is it an admission that the values of the automotive industry determine governmental priorities?

Another case in point: In the international arena, it is estimated that large cities will grow most rapidly in the Third World. One reason for this trend is the relationship in the Third World between authoritarian governments and the multinational corporations. This "enclave industrialization" has led to a premature urbanization with devastating social consequences for migrants from the land who find themselves unemployed and poorly sheltered. However a small group of Third-World elites and major stockholders of global corporations in North America and Europe are richly benefited by this policy. Left by the wayside are the poor and the hungry. Must the epitaph of every historical epoch read: "The strong did what they could and the weak suffered what they must?"

The answers, like the questions, become increasingly vague and distorted when the real moral issues are concealed by the obscurantism of lofty pronouncements. Realism is always in the interest of justice. Far too often, however, our notion of realism is merely a euphemism for self-interest. When we say "be realistic," we really mean "see it my way." The very people in the United States and Western Europe who espoused the virtues of foreign investment and belittled Third-World concerns about foreign control protested the loudest when OPEC nations used some of their surplus capital to acquire partial control over some Western corporations.

One essential aspect of justice and the enhancement of human rights is a more equitable redistribution of wealth between the rich and the poor societies. This will require, however, that realism determines rather than justifies the actions of government.

Human Rights in the Law and Romans (Series A)

Foster R. McCurley and John H. Reumann *

THE topic of "human rights" is not an easily defined concept in the lectionaries of the church. Human rights is not a special concern of the pericopes, and not a topic to which one can readily turn in the biblical books themselves. Rather, it is a modern theme and the preacher who wants to use the lessons to rouse a congregation to greater sensitivity for the oppressed and for justice in a repressive world will have to do some careful exegesis. Ways to connect this ethical concern with the Scriptures do exist, not least in some of Israel's law codes and in the epistles like Romans.

THE RISE OF THE "RIGHTS" PROBLEM

Actually, *human rights* is not a biblical term or even one from classical theology. It stems instead from the Enlightenment—"les droits de l'homme" is essentially a theme whose time came in the French and American Revolutions. As such, they are rights rooted in the assumptions of deism. And deism, in its concept of God and its view of human autonomy, was far removed from any notion of a God who acts in history or of people in bondage to sin or self, redeemed by Jesus Christ.

*The authors serve as Professors of the Old and New Testaments at the Lutheran Theological Seminary in Philadelphia.

BIBLICAL RESOURCES

There are, in fact, a whole series of areas where biblical thought relates to the modern concern for human dignity and rights. One such area has to do with God as Ruler. Biblical thought constantly assumes and states that over all creation, over all governments, human forces, and movements there rules a just God who will one day redress all the injustices of this life. He will repay those who mock the dignity of their fellow creatures; he will "put down the mighty from their thrones and exalt those of low degree" (Luke 1:52). Indeed, the Magnificat, referring to past mighty acts of God, states that he has already done this. So it is the disenfranchised who "cry to him day and night" (Luke 18:7) and the martyred who ask in hope, "Lord, how long?" (Rev. 6:10). This biblical view of God as judge of all is a powerful deterrent to inhuman conduct and a pressure toward justice.

The second area that may be mentioned is God's work in creation. God made all—every race, sex, type, color, and language of humanity. Even if we emphasize their fallen state, the fact remains that all people are his children by creation, giving them a particular and equal dignity. There are no stories about one race or another created with primacy or brought into existence disparagingly in Genesis 1—2. Woman is co-vicegerent, made simultaneously with man in Chapter 1 or at the other end of the ellipse of God's fashioning activity in Genesis 2.

The third area related to the theme of "equal in creation" is what is traditionally called God's providence, his care for all peoples. This care is so equal that at times the righteous protest that God is unfairly letting the wicked flourish. The God of the Scriptures gives "rains and fruitful seasons," satisfying "hearts with good and gladness" in "all the nations of the world" (Acts 14:17). As Jesus described God's beneficence, "Your Father who is in heaven makes his sun rise on the evil and on the good, and sends rain on the just and on the unjust" (Matt. 5:45).

We may also approach the matter from the standpoint of biblical anthropology. Fourth, then, is the matter of "the image of God." The statement in Genesis 1:26–27 that "God created man in his own image, in the image of God he created him; male and female he created them," can be traced to show that even after the Fall this image continued (Gen.5:1–3). It continued after the Flood, so that the statement "God made man in his own image" serves as a basis for condemning the murder of another human being (Gen. 9:6), in the "Noah-covenant" for all humanity.

The fifth related area dealing with human rights is that of proverbial wisdom. This oft-neglected area of biblical theology offers us the most pronounced concern for human rights. Wisdom, particularly that variety attested in the Book of Proverbs, begins with the assertion that the whole world is the creation of God and is established in an orderly way. Indeed creation is governed by an order which persons of insight can determine and live by. Thus, the goal of wisdom teaching is to share human experiences in such a way that the pupil will learn to avoid the snares of evil and walk in paths of righteousness.

The established order of proverbial wisdom includes controlling the temper, avoiding bad company, holding the tongue for the proper moment to speak, disciplining children, and so on. But it also insists that one treat others with justice—not because they are brothers or sisters in the faith or of like national identification, or because of cultic or folk laws—because everyone is a part of humanity sharing common experiences in God's creation.

Often, proverbial wisdom attempts to protect the human rights of the poor and needy simply because they have no means to protect themselves (see Prov. 14:21; 21:13; 22:9; 28:3, 27; 31:20). Indeed, a righteous person is one who "knows the rights of the poor" (29:7), and in caring for the needy, one is somehow performing the work of God himself (see Prov. 14:31; 17:5; 19:17; 22:22–23; 23:10–11). Even a king's stability on his throne is determined by how well he cares for the poor (see Prov. 29:14; cf. also v. 4).

In any case, for rich and poor alike, the insistence on human rights ranges from respect for the persons themselves to respect for the property they own. Therefore, proverbial wisdom repeatedly denounces the bearing of false witness against a fellow human being (see Prov. 19:5, 9, 28; 21:28; 25:18) and affirms the honor of keeping a person's secrets (see Prov. 11:12–13; 25:9–10). A person's property is also to be respected, whether inherited from former generations (see Prov. 22:28; 23:10) or purchased in one's lifetime (see Prov. 11:1; 20:10, 23).

Wisdom literature makes no pretensions about the limits of

human ability, action, and discretion. On the contrary, the proverbs emphasize the limitations of human life on the one hand and the complete sovereignty of God on the other (see Prov. 16:1, 9; 19:21; 20:23; 21:30f.). But precisely in recognizing God's sovereignty over all, the wisdom teachers asserted the dignity of every human being regardless of class, rank, nationality, or sex.

Before leaving the area of proverbial wisdom, we need to say a word about its role and significance for Christians. While the Book of Proverbs does not proclaim the gospel, and adherence to proverbial teaching will not lead to salvation, nevertheless proverbial wisdom is good for what it's good for! It helps us to live honorable lives and to make choices in matters that reason rather than faith determines. Thus proverbial wisdom should not be neglected by the church, but rather studied so that, in such areas as human rights, its contributions might be understood and appreciated.

For example, since wisdom teaching can be recognized as completely international in scope, the church need not insist that a particular form of government be a prerequisite for asserting human rights. If Israel, Egypt, Babylon, Edom, and Canaan taught very much the same proverbs, particularly in regard to the care of the poor, then likewise both American and Soviet forms of government are equally responsible and accountable for the dignity of the human beings under their control.

A sixth area of insight from the Bible is found in the commands of God, the law codes of Israel, and the imperatives or *paraenesis* ("admonition") in the New Testament. The "Ten Words" of Yahweh in Exodus 20 and Deuteronomy 5 can be regarded as advanced for their day, with implications for our day and the "human rights breakthrough" (as Walter Harrelson has argued in *The Ten Commandments and Human Rights*).

Several recent studies on the structure of the Decalogues, especially the Decalogue given at Sinai, have concluded that the ten laws actually fall into pairs dealing with five areas of life. The first three pairs deal with (1) the exclusivity and personality of God (Exod. 20:3–4), (2) the realm of holiness in which cult and Sabbath are preserved (Exod. 20:7–8), and (3) family life (Exod. 20:12, 14; the oldest manuscripts list these consecutively as a pair). The final two pairs move into the area of human rights: (4) the free life of the individual in terms of the prohibitions against killing (Exod. 20:13) and kidnapping (Exod. 20:15; "steal" seems to have referred originally to stealing a person) and (5) the protection of the fellow citizen in terms of his rights as a person (Exod. 20:16) and of his property (Exod. 20:17).

The last two pairs emphasize that social life and justice are dependent on the protection of an individual's freedom, rights and property. How appropriate it is to our discussion that in the Decalogue of God's will for Israel, two of the five pairs of laws are devoted to human rights! God's imperative here is based on the indicative that it was he who brought the people out of bondage in Egypt.

Other laws related to human rights are based on that same divine indicative. Perhaps Deuteronomy 25 expresses more humanitarian interest than any other single chapter in the Bible. Beginning at verse 10, the law protects the dignity of the person who borrowed something and offers a pledge. Verses 14–15 insist that a poor person be paid his wages the same day he earns them. Verse 17 prohibits the perversion of justice to the sojourner, orphan, and widow on the ground, "You were a slave in Egypt and the Lord God redeemed you from there" (v. 18). And finally the law insists on leaving some wheat, olives, and grapes in the fields after a harvest so that the sojourner, orphan, and widow might have something to eat (vv. 19–21). This humanitarian concern is based once again on the remembrance "that you were a slave in the land of Egypt" (v. 22).

Thus the human rights commanded in Israel's law codes— unlike those concerns expressed in proverbial wisdom—are based on the Lord's activity in history which made Israel his people. But even though the laws are addressed to his covenant people, God's will for justice extends far beyond Israel herself. Equality before the law is rooted in the impartiality of Yahweh, with whom there is "no respect for persons." (That KJV phrase, from the Greek root *prosopolempsia*, does not mean God fails to respect our personhood. It rather is a rendering of a Hebrew idiom, "to lift up the fact," and means "show partiality to," cf. James 2:1, 9; Acts 10:34, or that God is "impartial," 1 Peter 1:17.) For the New

Testament, an equivalent term for "law" or "right" (*mishpat*) is often "the will of God" (Rom. 2:17-18; 12:2). And his will, for us toward others, is often expressed in exhortations and commands.

Seventh, there is the theme of salvation, especially in the New Testament. In the Old Testament, God acted to deliver Israel, and there are only hints and scattered insights of redemption of the nations, though at times there are universal visions. In the New Testament, God's action in Christ is for all. The redeemed community is to break all barriers in its inclusive fellowship (Gal. 3:28), barriers of nationality (Jew, Greek), of economics and society (slave, free), of sexual discrimination (male, female). The movement is not centripetal, toward Jerusalem, but outward into God's world. The Christian concept of redemption has been a powerful force urging people to turn toward others—to share and accept them as equals. "Beneath the cross all the ground is level."

Finally, we must appeal, as the Vatican Declaration does and generations of preachers have, to the example of Jesus. He recognized human worth where contemporary religion did not always see it—in outcasts, publicans, harlots, the disenfranchised. He went to them, appealed to all, but in the meeting did not fail to recognize their rights and dignity.

All of these areas—God as Judge and Creator, Providence, the will and law of God, proverbial wisdom, humans as created and redeemed, and Jesus' ministry, can be points of contact for looking at human rights. And since the preacher is likely to find these recurrent emphases in passage after passage, once one begins to look for them, the possiblities for relating human rights and dignity to the pericopes are multiplied. Indeed, so basic a precept as the Golden Rule, "Whatever you wish that men would do to you, do so to them" (Matt. 7:12, parallel Luke 6:31) has within it the germ of equality in rights and dignity.

THE LECTIONARY, "A" CYCLE, PENTECOST

What can the lectionary preacher find in the Pentecost lessons as appointed? Year A of the Three-Year Lectionary calls for use of Matthew 11—21, Romans 7—14, and Philippians, plus a miscellany of Old Testament lessons related to the gospel passage for each day, in the months of July through September. If we add the remainder of the church year, the selections go on through Matthew 25 (the parables about the parousia and final judgment) and 1 Thessalonians. The following suggestions are made from the gospels for the day. In addition one can look for any of the themes noted above in the other lessons as well.

On 9 Pentecost, the Parable of the Wheat and the Tares is appointed, Matthew 13:24–30, with the possibility of reading 13:36–43, the allegorical explanation as well. The latter verses should certainly be studied in seeking Matthew's meaning. Within the ministry of Jesus, 13:24–30 can be read as a defense of Jesus' ministry to outcasts: God will make the judgment, at the end, meanwhile "let wheat and tares grow together." Allegorically, verses 36–43 apply the point to the church: God will separate the bad Christians from the good, but later on; such judgment is not our task. Both, so to speak, have equal rights to grow.

Thus Reginald Fuller, in *Preaching the New Lectionary*, sees "the forbearance of God" as the point of the day. The *Ordo* use of Wisdom 12:13, 16–19 makes that point stand out; Isaiah 44:6–8 in the Lutheran lectionary puts more emphasis on God as sovereign Lord and redeemer. A social justice emphasis could stress God's forbearance with us, implying our forbearance of others; Jesus' outreach to all, equally, with implications for us; and God as the ultimate Judge.

On 16 Pentecost we have in Matthew 18:15–17 three well-known steps for settling a dispute within the church community. The thrust is communal discipline. This is a good example of how Matthew balances openness toward the world and mission to all sorts of people (13:38; 28:19–20) with a strong insistence on the need for the church group to discipline itself. It is also an instance of how the church uses worldy wisdom (the three steps) for its own governance. What makes it the community of Jesus Christ is his presence "where two or three are gathered in his name" (vv. 19–20). The church emerges as that group around Christ, disciplining itself according to commonsense rules and techniques shared with the world for the sake of its mission. What do the demands for human rights throughout our world say to the church today?

Concerning the Parable of the Laborers in the Vineyard (Matt. 20:1–16) on 18 Pentecost, let us simply state that all commentators agree it is not wise to build economic policy of any sort on this passage. That would be incorrect social application. But if the point is to depict a generous, surprising God, who treats all justly and the most unlikely persons more generously than church people might suppose, what does that say about God's view of the dignity of those whom we may despise?

In *Proclamation,* J. T. Forestell sees the parable "in the ministry of Jesus" and "a rebuke to those Pharisees who would treat God according to the strict equality of justice." *Our* justice always enables us to come off better than others. *God's* justice is more gracious (cf. also Isaiah 55:6–11, the Old Testament appointment).

On 22 Pentecost we have the passage about Tribute Money (Matt. 22:15–21), about which a suggestion has already been made. And to anticipate the Last Sunday in the church year, the "Parable" of the Great Judgment (Matt. 25:31–46) may be a powerful pointer toward God's end-time surprises and God's will and plan for non-Christians. But that passage merits our fuller exposition in the next volume of *Justice.*

LESSONS FROM ROMANS

We would be remiss, however, if we did not recommend some attention to the epistles in this Pentecost period. Preachers have tended to focus on the gospel appointments the first time around, with occasional attention to the Old Testament lessons. But even if this is the second time you are following Series A, it is unlikely that the epistle for the day has been the basis for preaching. And, despite many studies to relate the epistle to the other lessons as a massive (and often ingenious) unity, the *Ordo's* own principle needs to be reiterated: the epistle selections generally move in their own sequence from week to week and do not have a necessary connection with the other two passages for the day.

From Trinity Sunday until 17 Pentecost we have an in-sequence reading of highlights from Paul's Epistle to the Romans. Those seventeen weeks make it the longest epistle sequence in the lectionary. Most of the appointed Romans passages, which begin with 3:21ff. on 2 Pentecost, are fairly brief. They are often doxological. Chapter 8, verses 8–9, is divided up over four consecutive Sundays. The most difficult portions of chapters 9–11 are not used and the ethical exhortations from chapters 12–14 are employed for four Sundays. Except for the total omission of 1:1—3:20, the lectionary's coverage of Romans is representative.

If one were looking for a time to do a series on an epistle of some length and importance, this is the appropriate time. Those who esteem Romans, but seldom expound it, ought to face the challenge now.

For those concerned with issues of justice/righteousness, the prominence of this theme as justification/God's righteousness in Romans is readily apparent. One may wish, in connection with human dignity, to do something with Labor Day, and in connection with the United Nations and human rights, the commemoration of Dag Hammarskjöld on September 18.

What specifically might be emphasized in preaching from Romans? In the overall argument one cannot escape the ideas, repeated like a tolling bell, of (a) the solidarity of humanity in sin and (b) the universality of redemption offered in Jesus Christ. (a) "All have sinned and fall short of the glory of God" (3:23), (b) "the righteousness of God has been manifested . . . for all who believe" (3:21–32); the gospel is "the power of God for salvation to every one who has faith" (1:16); Christ died for all the ungodly (5:6). All the world, Jew and Gentile alike, are under the power of sin (1:18—3:20); but where sin increased, grace abounded all the more (5:20). The twin themes of equality in sin before God and of salvation for all from God remove any of our own pretentions and put us in the same boat, sinking or rescued, with the rest of humanity. Herein lies a powerful appeal to see the worth and place of all others whom God made and for whom Christ died.

It is unfortunate for our concern that Romans 2:14–15, about how "Gentiles who do not have the law do by nature what the law requires," thanks to what is "written on their hearts," never appears in the Sunday or festival lectionary. Nevertheless, it deserves consideration. In Paul's day the passage must have been a powerful put-down for the Jew who vaunted himself over having the law (though he may not have obeyed it). In our day, how clearly it speaks against Christians who glory in their spiritual heritage (without especially exercising it) and look down on "the nations" of our time. Others, beside believers, may be doing what God's will calls for!

One passage which surely deserves treatment is Romans 13:1–10, about the Christian and the state, assigned for 16 Pentecost. The Lutheran lectionary has pointedly added the first seven verses to the *Ordo* choice of 13:8–10, in part because of a conviction that congregations need to hear about the state and the Christian's relation to government. The preacher ought to be challenged to wrestle with this text especially in the American or Canadian context.

One can safely set aside theories that Romans 13:1–7 is a post-Pauline insert. In its theme "be subject," it is similar to the common early Christian ethical codes found in 1 Peter, Colossians, Ephesians, and the Pastorals. Perhaps there are common Jewish Graeco-Roman backgrounds. We need to say however, that Romans 13 is not the sole New Testament passage on the state. Revelation 13 is a "no" to Rome; 1 Peter calls for reverence, even for the emperor, but warns of suffering. A full doctrine of church and state must be worked out contextually by the interpreter, with all these passages in mind.

Government, according to 13:3, 4, 6 is a minister of God "for good," i.e., for right and for justice. The novel effort to interpret government as an arm of the risen *Christ*, who rules it through angelic powers (on this view, "the powers that be" in the state) can be safely discarded, even though it has found its way into a few recent commentaries (Cranfield calls it "highly probable"; contrast Barrett and Käsemann). The suggestion from Marxsen and Leenhardt is intriguing: to render 13:8*b* "the person who loves has fulfilled 'the other law,' " i.e., the revealed law of Moses, in contrast to the civil law of Rome (13:1–7 plus 8*a*, "owe no one anything," pay your taxes, etc.), but it has scarcely won the day. To wrestle, however, with what it means to "love your neighbor" in a global village, where we cannot avoid dealing with the state and corporate powers, may be a springboard to talk about human rights.

Perhaps the most fascinating suggestion regarding social justice in these chapters comes on the previous Sunday, 15 Pentecost, when Romans 12:1-8 is read. This is the beginning of Paul's ethical section, calling for total response to God and his saving righteousness in everyday life, using all our grace-gifts and natural endowments. This leads us into the *charismata* (12:6) which members of the body of Christ need in order to operate with each other and with the world. The next to the last function in Paul's list deserves special attention, "he who gives aid, with zeal."

What is *ho proistamenos* supposed to do "with zeal"? Käsemann cites 1 Thessalonians 5:12 to suggest it means "organizational tasks." Others have found here the prototype of episcopal governance. The root is behind the description of Phoebe at Romans 16:2 as a "helper of many" and of Paul. The idea in classical Greek would be of a protector or supporter. But of what?

Some think this *proistamenos* has charge of the congregation's charitable work; the preceding and following references (v. 3) to the "carer of souls" who encourages or comforts, the "distributor" (or congregational treasurer), and the "mercyperson" who may have cared for the sick, visited prisoners, or buried the dead. In this context of "caring" ministries, Michel has suggested we have a function of befriending and protecting members of the community, like widows, orphans, slaves, etc., who were in no position to defend themselves. Was this a kind of first-century Christian ombudsman for those whose rights might be violated? C.E.B. Cranfield (p. 37, n. 1) asks whether parishes today might not use such a champion for those whose position is disadvantaged, like prisoners on parole, foreign workers, and the mentally defective. Does not the church also have a champion or advocacy role beyond the local parish?

We conclude this list of possibilities from Romans with a reference to the brief lesson from chapter 14, verses 7-9, on 17 Pentecost: "None of us lives to himself, none of us dies to himself" ("no man is an island," John Donne). "We are the Lord's" by redemption, all equally his daughters and his sons. This argument against isolationism because of our life together in Jesus Christ can be set in the context of this chapter—concerning "the strong" and "the weak." "Let us no more pass judgment on one another" (14:13). In a world where the weak seemingly get weaker and the strong more arrogant, what and how do the members of Christ's body speak out and act for the rights of others today?

OLD TESTAMENT PERICOPES

Among the Old Testament pericopes assigned for the quarter, several texts commend themselves for preaching on human rights. The sovereignty of God over all peoples on earth is reflected to a greater or lesser extent at 1 Kings 19:9–18 and Exodus 19:1–6. On 12 Pentecost the story of Elijah at Mount Horeb is a polemic both against Canaanite theophany theology and against the sanctity of places. But the address of God to Elijah in the last part of the story (1 Kings 19:15–18) commissions the prophet to anoint— among others—the new king of Syria. That the Lord's authority to appoint foreign kings is simply assumed by the story writer and is evidence of a common belief in God's universal reign.

At Exodus 19:1–6, designated for St. Bartholomew, Apostle, the assertion of God's universal authority is much more explicit. Here, in a covenant formula Israel is offered the possibility of becoming the Lord's personal treasure (RSV, "my own possession"), a kingdom of priests, and a holy nation. All these titles represent function as well as privilege, for they designate Israel as one who is separated from other nations in order to perform God's service among the nations as priests do within society. This function is given to Israel because "all the earth is mine" (v. 5). Thus God's care for all nations provides the motive for his election of Israel.

In light of this sovereignty of God and the mission he gave to Israel, it is not surprising that in the postexilic period, membership in the community of Israel was opened up for all. At Isaiah 56:1, 6–8 (13 Pentecost) an oracle from the Lord inaugurates a new era by inviting peoples formerly excluded from the worshiping community to "join themselves to the Lord" (v. 6). Verses 3–5, omitted in the lectionary, allow both eunuchs and foreigners to join the community; thus they reverse the law at Deuteronomy

23:1-8 which prohibited these groups from entering the Lord's assembly. The verses selected for the lectionary make explicit that membership in the worshiping community is no longer a matter of nationality.

It is now a choice by an individual to confess the Lord as God, to minister to him, love him, serve him, and to keep the sabbath and hold fast his covenant. Thus all exclusiveness—so prominent in the reforms of Ezra and Nehemiah—is rejected by this new order in which the gates of fellowship are opened to the world.

On 19 Pentecost the lesson from Ezekiel 18:25-29 indicates that the person who acts rightly according to natural law shows more righteousness than the house of Israel who questions the justice of the Lord. Thus the prophet of the exile appeals to a sense of justice in which every individual in the human race is responsible for his or her behavior.

The climax to the Joseph story, Genesis 50:15-21 (17 Pentecost), offers a unique opportunity to deal with the issue of human rights. Gerhard von Rad has demonstrated that the Joseph story is a didactic wisdom story containing those characteristics of wisdom discussed above. The point of the whole story can be summed up in Joseph's words to his penitent brothers: "You meant evil against me; but God meant it for good, to bring it about that many people should be kept alive, as they are today" (Gen. 50:20). The limitations of human knowledge are confirmed, for what is stressed is the mysterious divine control of events by which God can work good out of the evils done by humans. The "good" done by God in this story is the feeding of many people, mostly foreign Egyptians, by his use of a man named Joseph. This demonstrates not only God's love for all his creatures but also the dignity of the persons he created.

Thus, in the manner of proverbial wisdom, the Joseph story affirms God's providential and mysterious care for those who are unable to care for themselves. And at the same time this didactic wisdom piece has become part of the history of God's relationship with his people which originated with his promise to Abraham and came to fulfillment "in Christ Jesus whom God made our wisdom" (1 Cor. 1:30).

FURTHER READINGS
ON ROMANS

Barrett, C. K. *Reading through Romans.* (Philadelphia: Fortress, 1977.)
Helpful for a quick review with a lay study group.
_____. *The Epistle to the Romans.* Harper's New Testament Commen-
taries. (New York: Harper & Row, 1957). No longer the newest or
most detailed, but reliable. (As soon as available, secure the English
translation of the recent major commentary by Ernst Käsemann).
Cranfield, C.E.B. *A Critical and Exegetical Commentary on the Epistle
to the Romans.* International Critical Commentary Series. Vol. 1, In-
troduction and Romans I–VIII (Edinburgh: T & T Clark, 1975).
_____. *A Commentary on Romans 12–13.* Scottish Journal of Theology,
Occasional Papers No. 12 (Edinburgh: Oliver and Boyd, 1965). A full-
scale treatment, first in the new round of ICC volumes, by a New
Testament editor, like Barrett at Durham. Barthian overtones.

ON OLD TESTAMENT

Harrelson, Walter. *The Ten Commandments and Human Rights.* Over-
tures to Biblical Theology. (Philadelphia: Fortress, 1978).
von Rad, Gerhard. *Wisdom in Israel.* (Nashville: Abingdon, 1972).
Westermann, Claus. *Isaiah 40–66.* The Old Testament Library.
(Philadelphia: Westminster, 1969).

Theology, Politics, and Human Rights

Richard J. Niebanck

THERE'S a story going around Eastern Europe about a Czech and a Polish dog who happen to meet at the border between their respective countries.

The Czech dog asks his Polish cousin, "Why are you going to Czechoslovakia?"

"To eat," replies the Pole. In turn, he puts it to the Czech: "And why, may I ask, would you be going to Poland?"

"To bark," answers the Czech.

This little anecdote expresses at least two-thirds of the "human-rights debate" as it is currently being waged. On the one hand, there is the Western liberal-democratic tradition—"the freedom to bark"—and, on the other, the stance of the (now not so monolithic) community of socialist countries—"the freedom to eat."

The fact that the joke comes from Eastern Europe suggests that the debate about "barking" versus "eating" exists not only *between* the so-called capitalist and socialist camps but within each one as well. The ongoing debate within the United States over the issues of guaranteed employment, income, housing, and health care reflects the presence of many whose needs are not answered by the mere "freedom to bark." Whether these *needs* are in fact *rights* which a society is obligated to guarantee is precisely what is at issue.

The third party to the human-rights debate is that disparate group of newer nation-states of the "Third World" (an appellation rapidly losing acceptability with them). Members of this group may look "eastward" or "westward" (though geograph-

ically almost always northward) for political and economic support. Yet, albeit with differing overtones, they all ring the
changes on another category of "human rights"—the self-determination of peoples.

Popular self-determination is hardly a new thing under the
sun. It was articulated as one of Wilson's Fourteen Points; and it
claims as one of its ancestors the American struggle for independence from Britain. Now it has finally come into its own as
the rallying cry of a vast array of nations and would-be nations
and has won its place in the international rhetoric of human
rights. It is worth noting that, like so many other rhetorical
terms, the "self" in "self-determination" lacks (conveniently or in-
conveniently as the case may be) precise definition.

These developing nations are continually weighing the relative
merits of a capitalist or socialist "road" to modernization, at times
electing elements of each. Very few of these nations, however,
have undertaken to emulate the Western liberal democracy in the
establishment of democratic institutions and the formation of a
civil culture; and it is safe to say that in those cases where they
have, democratic rights are enjoyed by a small minority who oc-
cupy a place of relative economic privilege.

Where a "capitalist" approach is chosen, distributive justice/
economic rights usually get low priority; where a "socialist" approach is chosen, social justice ranks higher. In the latter case,
there is nevertheless a tremendous gap between declared intention and what is in fact delivered. And in too many instances,
whatever a country's orientation may be, there is often an over-
riding expenditure of resources on the maintenance of a modern
military.

REVEALED IDEOLOGY

Christians in the West, and in America particularly, have tended to view the bundle of democratic rights and institutions as if
they were a direct revelation from God. The positing of "self-
evident truths" and the viewing of rights as "certain" (in the sense
of a finite number), "inalienable" endowments by the Creator fits
well with the pious belief in plenary inspiration. So the American
state documents function in civil religion as Holy Writ and

philosophical "self-evidence" as revelation. The result is an ideological piety in which the Declaration of Independence and Constitution, like the Bible, become icons to be venerated rather than human documents to be critically understood.

Throughout the country's history, many Christians in the United States (with some notable exceptions) enthusiastically supported the marketing of "freedom." They failed to see that American foreign policy was frequently an imperialistic one, albeit wrapped in the flag of democratic idealism. From the Spanish-American War through the "Four Freedoms" to the Vietnam War, many American Christians sincerely believed that they were engaged in the advancement (or safeguarding) of democracy.

The admixture of democratic ideology and the Christian gospel has been especially evident in the history of American Christian influence in the Far East. There was, for instance, the complex relationship—personal, religious, political—between Chiang Kai-shek and American Protestantism. A more recent example is that of the involvement of prominent American Catholics in the shaping of U.S. policy regarding Vietnam following World War II. Describing that involvement, Robert Scheer writes:

> The Cardinal (Spellman) became one of Diem's most influential backers in the United States and there is no doubt that this support was crucial for, among other things, it certified Diem as an important anti-Communist—no small matter during the McCarthy period.[1]

The two decades of the Cold War gave a Manichaean cast to the American world view. On the one side were arrayed the "Children of Light," the nations of the "Free World" in the West; on the other stood the "Children of Darkness," those nations that had been "enslaved by Communism." This world view was nurtured and reinforced at both the popular and the sophisticated level by the American Christian community. As Secretary of State under Eisenhower, John Foster Dulles, a prominent Protestant layman, contributed heavily to both the shaping of that world view and the administering of the policies flowing from it.

The admixture of theology and democratic ideology was also

1. *How the United States Got Involved in Vietnam*, by Robert Scheer. (Fund for the Republic, Inc., 1965), p. 14.

manifest during that period in the public statements of the Commission of the Churches on International Affairs of the World Council of Churches. Dr. O. Frederick Nolde, who directed the Commission during those years, noted in retrospect that the Commission concerned itself with "freedom of opinion and expression across all frontiers; freedom of assembly and association . . . ; education, family and the prior right of parents to the education of their children; and in freedom from the retroactive application of penal law." Such rights as these were considered by the Commission to "make religious liberty meaningful."[2]

Thus religious liberty was, during that period, the centerpiece of Christian thinking about human rights; and such liberty was defined in essentially liberal-democratic terms.

The thought patterns instilled during the Cold War are still strikingly evident in the contours of the American mind. There seems to be scant awareness on the part of the American public that the "Free World" is in large measure unfree. Military dictatorships which depend for their survival on American support maintain themselves through systematic brutality and torture. The poor in their countries are disenfranchised both economically and politically. There is neither "freedom to eat" nor "freedom to bark." The democratic niceties which the "Free World" is allegedly about are all but unknown.

RIGHTEOUSNESS, JUSTICE, AND "THE HUMAN"

Historic evangelical theology does not proclaim self-evident truths or a quantum of discrete entitlements handed to persons by a Creator otherwise removed from the world. Nor does evangelical theology proclaim a message of economic determinism or a social theory in which the person is nothing while the collectivity is all in all. It eschews the celebration of nationalisms in which everyone serves an abstract "general will" in the name of self-determination of peoples.

But, against these ideologies of "First,'" "Second," and "Third" world, evangelical theology says not so much a resounding, "No," as a critical, "Yes, but . . ."

2. *Free and Equal*, by O. Frederick Nolde, (Geneva: World Council of Churches, 1968) pp. 54, 38.

"Yes," in the sense that a legitimate set of human concerns is reflected, in however truncated a form, in the particular ideological formation; "but," in the sense that other equally legitimate (and perhaps more urgent) human concerns and needs are systematically being overlooked by the ideology and the policies flowing from it.

Christian theology proclaims a holy God whose righteousness stands in judgment over every ideology and every form of social organization.

Justice is the response which the righteous God requires of the human creation. Such justice is seen as active *doing:* answering the concrete needs of all members of the human family. Doing justice is the exercise of responsible stewardship of the power and resources which God has entrusted to humankind.

The justice God demands is inclusive. It reflects the inclusive righteousness, the universal power and love of the Creator. The stranger and sojourner, the weak and the widowed, are *in,* not out. God demands that society attend to their needs, not out of charity, but out of justice. It is an act of blasphemy to declare anyone as being outside the human family, "less human" or "less equal" before God. Distinctions by and among humans are at best provisional and always subject to change or removal. The only absolute distinction is that between the Creator and the creation.

Justice is to be done within the human community. Human persons are constituted by their relationships—to God and to one another. Neither the person nor the group is primary: persons are created together in *co*-humanity, *com*-unity. It is in this situation that the God-given capacity for mutuality, reciprocity, empathy, and answerability emerges as an essential mark of "the human." Charles Williams's characterization of the believing community is no less apt as a description of God's intention for humanity: "co-inherence," referring to the unity of humankind, and "exchange," referring to the individuality of persons and the interaction between and among them.

Humanity is further understood psychosomatically. Persons are animated bodies, not spirits imprisoned in flesh. Human "co-inherence and exchange" is both symbolic and physical; and it is fundamentally sexual (two becoming one flesh). Justice therefore involves the meeting of physical need as well as the need of symbolic expression. "Eating" and "barking" are both essential to being a "dog."

Finally, human existence is historical in character. The human reality is always "in process," developing new ways of interrelation, new configurations of social life and meaning. There is no fixed body of rights or obligations revealed for all time. There is, however, a fundamental obligation of any generation not to deprive generations to come of the possibility of pursuing "the human project" (Gibson Winter)—discovering for themselves what God's intention implies.

THE GIFT OF REASON

Reason is the God-given endowment by which humanity is enabled to discern within specific historical contexts what justice requires. Reason is here understood not as the repository of *a priori* truths but as the capacity to perform certain functions (e.g. analysis, categorizing, generalizing, synthesizing). The Aristotelian legacy, as mediated by Thomas Aquinas, has, for instance, given a number of useful concepts which have served well in determining the form and content of justice (civil righteousness).

1) *Types of justice.* The tradition identifies three types of justice: commutative, distributive, and legal. Daniel C. McGuire describes these as follows:

> Commutative justice renders what is due in relationships between individuals; distributive justice directs the fair distribution of goods and burdens to the citizens by those who represent the state; legal justice represents the debts of the individual to the social whole or the common good. In each case persons are rendering what is due to others.[3]

2) *Characteristics of a just law.* A just law is described in this tradition as an ordinance of reason (formal cause) for the common good (final cause) made by the rightly constituted authority (efficient cause) and promulgated (material cause). This formulation sets forth both the end of justice—the common good—and

---

3. "Unequal But Fair," by Daniel C. McGuire. *Commonweal*, October 14, 1977, p. 649.

the just way in which legislation is in fact enacted. It says that just legislation should not be arbitrary (that is, it should be an ordinance of reason); that is should be enacted publicly (promulgated); and that such enactment should be done by the duly constituted agency having "the care of the commonwealth."

3) *The tests of a just law.* Finally, this tradition gives three tests of just legislation or policy: (a) it should be directed at remedying a genuine social ill or accomplishing a legitimate social end; (b) it should be enforceable; and (c) it should not have side effects that destroy the end intended or create conditions worse than the ill to be remedied.

THE REALITY OF SIN

All that has been said thus far about human nature and the human capacity to ascertain the requirements of justice must be seen through an "overlay" of radical estrangement or, in more classically Christian terms, original sin. Through such an "overlay" God's intention of "co-inherence and exchange" for the human community is broken into a false individualism on the one hand and a false collectivism on the other. It is against such a bifurcation that Christians contend as they participate in the political struggle for human rights. They seek to advance personal and communal justice that is grounded in the divine intention and not distorted by self-serving rationalization and ideologizing.

McGuire states the matter extremely well:

No one form of justice can be stressed to the point of repressing another form. All three serve in concert to create the basis for moral existence. If you fixate on commutative justice, and this is the American penchant, you have an atomistic, social concept of personhood. On the other hand, a radically collective anthropology would down-play commutative justice and submerge the individual into the collectivity. Pure collectivism and pure individualism do not exist, but operant biases can be discerned, as in American individualism or in Maoist collectivism. Both biases seek an unnatural release from the essential paradoxical tension between individual and social claims.[4]

4. Ibid.

HUMAN RIGHTS: JUSTICE MADE SPECIFIC

Given the view of human nature outlined above, theology finds itself closer to those who consider human rights to be a provisional specification of justice within a socio-historical context than to those who would search for a body of universal and "nonconflictable" human rights. At the same time, drawing on its understanding of sin, and making maximum use of such rational principles as the ones mentioned earlier, theological ethics would be vigilant regarding the tendency of the powerful to define their own privileges in terms of rights, and the universal human tendency to cloak appetite in the language of rights (as in the rhetoric of self-fulfillment). Theological ethics recognizes the need to guard against giving false legitimacy to inherently unjust power relationships and the policies flowing from them. The refinement and application of tests such as those of fairness or equity are important in this connection.

What are commonly called human rights come into being essentially as a response to definite historical conditions. As such they function in one or another of the following ways:

1) As claims to protection against/liberation from perceived oppression by economic, political, or social/cultural power; and
2) claims to a just share of (usually newly-generated) wealth or opportunity.

The claim for liberation and/or protection may be against hitherto unchallenged political, social, or economic relations which have lately been "discovered" by emergent groups possessed of new power and self-consciousness. So the nobility challenged the English king at Runnymede, producing in Magna Carta, principles which became fundamental to the British concept of justice and law; so did the emerging bourgeoisie challenge the "divine" or "natural" right of monarchs, replacing it with "the right of the people" to "alter or abolish" unjust government (Declaration of Independence). The Declaration of the Rights of Man, and the specific legal formulations of civil and political rights guaranteed by the constitutions of the liberal democracies are "residuals" of that moment in Western history.

On the other hand, claims to protection/liberation may be

against new, and potentially dangerous or tyrannical modes of production, economic organization, or government. The rights embedded in the rhetoric of the various labor movements— particularly the right to bargain collectively—are examples. The interests and needs of the working person have been articulated by the trade union movement within the industrialized countries and, through political pressure, have been translated into legal entitlements and protections. On the world scene, e.g., the International Labor Organization (ILU) has been a strong advocate of the rights of workers and has taken leadership in articulating standards and rights which could have applied to various national settings. As of yet, however, there has been developed no significant political power to make these standards effective.

The specification of human rights stands midway between the articulation of general principles of justice and the actual conversion of those principles into legislation. Human rights are the stuff of declarations and manifestos; they are in effect heralds of entitlements and protections that eventually may be guaranteed by law. They are part of the raw material of legislation, and they function as standards which judge the policies and behavior of governments, corporations, and other agents of power over the lives of people. They also call into question the accepted value systems and cultural stereotypes which mirror unjust power relationships (e.g. between men and women).

The process of articulating human rights is provisional and untidy. Participating in it are the self-serving as well as the idealistic. Groups of different kinds take part: highly organized bodies representing very specific sets of issues (e.g. labor unions and consumer advocacy groups), groups and coalitions advancing a wider spectrum of claims, and "humanitarian" groups and organizations which in many cases articulate and advance the rights of those who, by virtue of their powerlessness or political subjugation, are unable to speak for themselves.

The fact that a right is claimed by a particular interest group does not in and of itself invalidate that claim; nor does the articulation of a right by an apparently disinterested group of "humanitarians" guarantee that claim's legitimacy. Whether a claim deserves the status of a right is determined within the situation of assertion-counter-assertion that characterizes the human-rights enterprise. The "time" for certain rights "comes" as the pressure of circumstances creates the necessary political conditions. Those who engage in the human-rights enterprise must, therefore, attend as much to the development and use of political power as to the clear and credible articulation of the rights themselves.

THE CHURCH AND HUMAN RIGHTS

The church possesses two normative characteristics which, whenever they are actualized, make the community of the faithful a unique participant in the work of articulating human rights, creating political conditions that are supportive of these rights, securing their conversion into appropriate legislation, and minimizing their violation. These characteristics are:

1) The tangible spatial-temporal existence of the church in particular places; and
2) the universality of the church that transcends humanly-imposed barriers such as those of race, nation, interest, and class.

The first of these characteristics puts the church *where the people are* in their daily lives with their many tensions, conflicts, burdens, and contradictions. The church in a particular place is positioned to *know* the specific needs of the people, to help in the articulation of those needs, and to advocate policies which answer them in ways that are germane and not cosmetic.

A grass-roots organization in the fullest sense, the local church can do much to help people perceive what their true needs and interests are and provide them with the support and encouragement they need in advancing their claims within the political process. It can function as an agent of empowerment in a way in which few other organizations can.

The second characteristic assures the church a self-correcting pluralism within its own life; it also gives the church access to communication that is not controlled by any single regime or special interest. The worldwide community of faith thus becomes a unique network of caring and prophetic criticism with a credibility based upon the fact that the church is ruled by none but its Lord. The fact that some regimes seek to curb the church is itself testimony to the fact that the church is possessed of a unique kind of power.

There are innumerable ways in which the church can act in behalf of humans and their rights. Among these are:

1) *Declaring the essential unity of the human person (the unity of "eating" and "barking") in community, and demanding policies which assure justice to the whole person and the whole body politic.* In America, for instance, this would mean once and for all the establishment of the rights to employment, income, housing, health care, and education as basic entitlements to every citizen.

2) *Declaring the role of the state to be that of servant to human welfare and security.* "The state is created for man, not man for the state." The church is steadfastly opposed to any regime which sets out to "save" citizens or to create a "new humanity." In the context of a socialist or a developing society, this would mean that the church, while standing in "critical solidarity" with the body politic as it seeks the goals of social justice, would resist any tendency on the state's part to require allegiance of an ultimate kind or to employ against its opponents means, whether gross (torture or terror) or subtle (thought control and brainwashing) that destroy persons and human community.

3) *Living out its transnational, trans-ethnic character.* This would involve an even stronger commitment on the part of the church to participate within the community of world organizations dedicated to the developing of international standards of justice and holding nations and other interests accountable before them. For the American churches, it would include, e.g., advocating the United States' return to active participation in the International Labor Organization.

CONCLUSION

In his often-quoted address to the Maryknoll sisters in New York in 1970, Julius K. Nyerere, president of Tanzania, declared:

Let us be quite clear about this. If the Church is interested in man as an individual, it must express this by its interest in the society of which those individuals are members. For men are shaped by the circumstances in which they live. If they are treated like animals, they will act like animals. If they are denied dignity, they will act without dignity. If they are treated solely as a dispensable means of production, they will become soulless hands, to whom life is a matter of doing as little work as possible and then escaping into the illusion of happiness and pride through vice.[5]

Human beings do not exist as separate atoms with "rights of property and property in rights" (Locke). They exist in responsible co-humanity, in a web of relationships with an ever-growing set of rights and responsibilities. Into such life-in-relationship they have been called by God. It is for the church to proclaim and work for the justice that such a life demands.

5. "The Church and Society," by Julius K. Nyerere. In *Freedom and Development*, (Oxford University Press, 1973), p. 228.

Congregational Life

Clergy Mediates in School Strike

A TEACHERS' strike had Concord, California in turmoil. Most of the teachers were on the picket line in California's tenth largest district. Substitutes kept classes open but students were disappointed at the cancellation of all athletics and music programs.

The news carried stories of mounting tensions. Some parents sympathized with the teachers. Others did not, bringing children to classes and shouting angrily at the pickets who shouted back. One of the parents badly injured a picket with his car. Administrators felt the anguish. One suffered a heart attack and died on the way to work. A teachers' union mediator suffered a nervous breakdown. Through all this a mediator for the state sought a solution in vain.

Local clergy met to see what might be done. One proposed that the group send a statement urging mediation to both sides and also to the press. This was approved, and sent to the teachers, the district, and the media. The two sides acknowledged it but the news was buried by the first injunction against the teachers.

Four days later Presbyterian Bob Christiansen phoned his Lutheran neighbor, Ross Hidy, to suggest that the two pastors make a direct and personal approach. He said, "Check with Bob Griswold of the union and see if he would talk with us." Hidy reported back quickly: "He's in his office waiting." On the way over they agreed to suggest a "Memo of Understanding" with a three-person panel to make a recommendation to bring peace. The teachers welcomed them and their ideas. They found Superintendent Jim Slezak just as positive. A draft the clergy

43

wrote was read to both sides. They agreed to meet the next morning and sign the agreement. Things had moved quickly.

The pastors located the mediator and shared the news. "You mean both sides are ready to approve this Memo?" He was surprised and cautious. "That's right, and they want to meet tomorrow and sign it." He responded at once: "Up to now we could not do this, the fifteen-day time period was not over. It *is* today! I'll propose this tomorrow!"

Though it was five o'clock the day was not over. The two clergymen spent four hours that night with Board Chairperson Edith Draemel encouraging her to be a leader with a spirit of trust. But four other board members could not be reached. The Superintendent, Dr. Jim Slezak, and another administrator would represent the district.

Friday morning did not go smoothly. The teacher's team was on hand early. The district team was being discouraged by their own legal counsel who, with the mediator, was at the court awaiting a session. They hoped the judge would order the teachers back to the classroom. The lawyer advised caution. But the teachers, who had believed they were to sign the "Memo," had called a meeting at two o'clock to consider voting to return to teaching. It was an odd situation.

The pastors reminded the district they had in good faith promised to approve the "Memo." Nothing happened, so the pastors said, "You leave us no alternative. We are going to call a press conference and announce that you have gone back on your word to work for peace." It was strong but it worked. They met and verbally approved the "Memo." They said they would sign after counsel had checked the phrasing. Then things really moved quickly.

The judge heard that the teachers were meeting at two o'clock and held over the session. At two o'clock after hearing of the "Memo" and the plan for a panel, the teachers voted joyfully to return to classes on Monday. This vote was relayed to the judge. On hearing it he observed, "Our being here is rather irrelevant. Let's go home!" The district principals heard the news from Dr. Jim Slezak, who described the plan and thanked the clergy for playing an important role. It was time to meet and sign the "Memo."

As the group was entering the room the mediator called the clergy aside and refused them admittance. "But both sides have asked us to be present!" "I'm very sorry. If you insist and go into the room, then I shall not enter." The pastors accepted but promised to check the propriety of his ruling.

It took but a few moments to sign the "Memo." As the news of the plan was announced, relief and joy swept through the area. Headlines in a Sunday paper told "How Two Ministers Ended the Strike." But it was not really "ended," only a truce, and not all was peaceful.

Many teachers who had not struck were anxious about the next Monday. One of them, a manual arts teacher, was very apprehensive. On Sunday he disappeared and was declared missing. Hikers found his dead body ten days later on Mt. Diablo, a revolver at his side.

When trouble developed on naming the panel's third person, a meeting of the group was called by the pastors. Five hours were needed to resolve the problems. The "Memo" was amended. Six new points would guide further actions. The panel was appointed, and in an intense week of hearings they gathered information and released their report. It did not bring harmony. They did review priorities and recommended setting aside $1,108,409 to enable "salary increases among all district employees found appropriate by the board." The teachers were not pleased: "*Teachers* were the panel's concern . . . not others."

The board's position was stated clearly at the outset of its long-awaited meeting: "We feel that the strike was not legal and that the teachers ought not be rewarded for striking." Floor comments were permitted and revealed polarization, in some cases even hatred. The two clergy brought greetings and asked for reconciliation and harmony. To no avail. The board in its review of the budget lines cut back the figure to half. As it chopped the figures the teachers were astonished. "Did you know this was going to happen?" they asked the ministers. "No! You heard us ask for favorable consideration of the report."

It became evident the clergy were in a bind. To be silent would seem to support the board. They agreed to ask for persmission to say a few words. Permission was granted. Their brief comments were at one point interrupted by a board member. Each asked for caution and perhaps for a tabling of the action to permit consultation now with the panel. The board refused, and passed their motion. In defense of their action they said, "The three who signed had no authority to commit the board to any action." Teachers seemed to feel betrayed. All were disappointed. The hopes of many were now dashed to pieces.

The teachers refused the board's offer but did stay in class. Only classroom duties were to be accepted, no extra assignments. The mood was unpleasant. One school principal, writing to thank the clergy noted,

> I have never seen a happier, more cooperative group of teachers following the signed agreement between the two groups . . . teachers were teaching, coaches were coaching, and the bands were marching. Everything was so beautiful! It is hard to conceive that the morale of the faculty could move from heights like that to where it fell following the board meeting the 13th. The most healthful climate conducive to a learning atmosphere is a classroom with a positive attitude on the part of the teacher . . . I only hope that time will heal the feelings and attitudes that so drastically changed in one short evening.

At this writing, there is still a stand-off. A recall movement is under way for the entire board, further polarizing the community. True, an effort is being made to re-establish communications, but we see the board holding firm. The students are suffering.

What have we learned? A number of things. Mediation is not as easy as some think. Getting involved takes hours of work. And the complexity of the issues is soon evident. Inflation has made work of school boards almost impossible. Income is rather fixed but costs rise. Vandalism costs thousands in some districts. And arson fires are not uncommon. Some citizens feel strongly that a person serving in a public position does not have a right to go on strike. Some talk of legislation to take tenure from anyone who strikes— police, firemen, and teachers, too.

One lives with news media often distorting developments. One brief quote on a newscast often seems slanted, distorted. If we heard a full interview we might get a balance but rarely in any short quote.

Some of the area pastors were unhappy. "We all worked but you are the ones who got the publicity." We showed carefully worded news releases representing the entire religious community. It did not help in some cases. Pastors are human, too. And some people felt we took the teachers' side. We didn't. The pastors were asked to come to be thanked, and our picture was published receiving the thanks of the teachers, but no report of our request for some caution on their part. Getting involved means getting criticized.

We did receive many phone calls and letters of appreciation. One lady sent each of our churches a hundred dollar "Thank you!"

We kept in close touch as we went along. We tried to relax, to let things unfold. We met, planned, evaluated, kept notes (two bulging folders of papers) and never spoke without checking on the other's perspective. We learned that previous contacts in a community are priceless. There's an informal power network in a community that helps get things done. Those who have been active in the community before are more effective in a crisis.

Our task was to be enablers, facilitators, healers, and listeners. We refused to be discouraged, and even when it did look hopeless we tried to be positive. There is a reservoir of good will in those praying Christians whom God is ready to work through now. One letter put it, "It is the heart of the church's mission to bring healing, particularly when wounds have been felt by all parties . . . There are many wounds to heal, some very deep."   R.F.H.

National Council on Human Rights

The National Council of the Churches of Christ in the U.S.A. speaks and acts frequently in behalf of human rights. Some feel that it speaks and acts too frequently and that is tends to represent a "liberal" point of view which does not reflect the thinking of major portions of the constituency of its member churches. Nevertheless, some significant utterances and actions do issue from this ecumenical agency. Examples can be found in the one policy statement and the several resolutions on human-rights issues which were adopted by the NCCC Governing Board on November 11, 1977.

The policy statement, which in NCCC practice carries basic authority, is on Southern Africa. An introductory section sets forth the theological context, the history and specifics of the current situation, and previous relevent actions of the National Council. Then it declares support for positive actions in Namibia, South Africa, the Zimbabwe (Rhodesia).

The recommended actions are directed toward (1) achieving majority rule in those nations, (2) eliminating governmental policies and practices which oppress segments of the publications, (3) assisting refugees, political prisoners, and others who suffer because of the denial of human rights, and (4) urging the United Nations, the United States government, and multinational corporations to use their influence for justice in Southern Africa. The statement also calls upon the United States government, (5) "to give strong support to the United Nations Decade for Action to Combat Racism and Racial Discrimination."

The Governing Board at the same meeting also approved several resolutions on human-rights issues, which were based on a policy statement called "Human Rights," which had been adopted by the National Council's General Assembly on December 6, 1963.

One of these resolutions speaks to the questions of religious and political suppression within the Soviet Union. Because of its relationship to the subject matter of Dr. George Brand's paper, this resolution is quoted in full:

> Recently the Soviet leaders and their allies have celebrated the 60th anniversary of the Bolshevik Revolution. We, the members of the Governing Board of the National Council of the Churches of Christ in the U.S.A., remember with sorrow but also with deep gratitude all martyrs who lost their lives for their faith in God and/or their love of freedom during that violent period of Russian history.
>
> While the Soviet government did not include in its amnesty proclaimed on this special occasion the prisoners of conscience, we appeal to President Breshnev to release, in the spirit of Helsinki all im-

prisoned Baptists, Catholics, Jews, Moslems, Orthodox, and other believers as well as political dissenters.

We appeal to all religious communities in the U.S.A. to pray and to act for the confessing Church, for all prisoners of conscience in the U.S.S.R. and other countries under Soviet domination, and for all victims of oppression wherever and by whomever they are being persecuted.

We also appeal to President Carter to continue to pursue vigorously his policy of human rights everywhere, including our own country.

By our prayers and actions let us assure our oppressed brothers and sisters everywhere that their plight is one of our foremost concerns and priorities.

The Governing Board also affirmed support of the rights of the NCC's appointed staff to organize and engage in collective bargaining. It urged approval of the new Panama Canal Treaties, of the setting of 1979 as the International Year of the Child, and of effective steps in and among the denominations to stress the dignity of handicapped persons and to enable them to participate fully in church and society.

The board asked President Carter to consider the commutation of the sentences of the remaining four Puerto Rican Nationalists who have been jailed since the 1954 shooting incident in the U.S. House of Representatives (the sentence of a fifth had already been commuted). The resolution ends with the statement that this "is not to be construed as approval of the actions of the aforesaid persons or of terrorist activities in general."

The board expressed support for the National Women's Conference held November 18-21, 1977 in Houston, Texas, urging the delegates "to give prayerful consideration to all issues which affect the lives of women—economic, social, cultural, and political—toward the end of identifying barriers which prevent women from full participation and equality in all aspects of national life and international life, and developing recommendations for means by which such barriers can be removed."

The governing body affirmed the boycott of products of J. P. Stevens to persuade that corporation to correct its unfair labor practices in accordance with the law and the directives of the National Labor Relations Board.

Finally, the board passed a resolution on the support of Indian people in their struggle against organizations threatening Indian nations and communities. This was the basis for urging the President, Congress, and state legislators to guarantee equal access to legal abortions through government funding.   C. W. T.

Cesar Chavez and J. P. Stevens

The struggle for justice and human rights is often seen as applying primarily to Communist bloc countries or to those nations whose governments are authoritarian and repressive. Dr. Brand's article (p. 14) reminds us that a "meaningful policy of human rights cannot only be concerned with external problems. A Western criticism of Soviet repression must also take into account those instances where human rights are violated within Western boundaries."

We are reminded in the same article that a "U.S. Helsinki Committee could point to the continuing denial of human rights to agricultural workers in this country . . . " (p. 14). In this instance, the concern is over economic injustices as well as violations of political and civil rights. The case in point, of course, had to do with Cesar Chavez and the United Farm Workers Union. Their struggle for the right to organize and negotiate labor contracts with California growers had been long and costly. Area churches and regional judicatories in the U.S. West and Southwest continue to affirm and assist the farm-worker cause. This was especially true a year ago when the religious community advocated strongly for passage of the California Agricultural Labor Relations Act which secured the right of farm workers to organize.

Another case of growing concern and involvement is the fifteen-year struggle by workers of the J. P. Stevens textile industry to assert their right to bargain collectively.

In 1974 the Textile Workers Union won the right to do this in an election among 3,400 Stevens workers in Roanoke Rapids, North Carolina. To this day the Union (now the Amalgamated Clothing & Textile Workers Union) and J. P. Stevens have been unable to reach a contract agreement. Because the company has had a history of labor and civil rights violations and because it continues to block or thwart organizing efforts among the mill workers, the union has launched a consumer boycott of Stevens products.

Southern judicatories of major church denominations have responded to the controversy. Conferences and consultations have been held, giving opportunity for church leaders and textile employers and employees to discuss the issues and probe the complexities of the situation. In some instances such gatherings, though regional in focus, have been ecumenical in participation.

It is evident that strong positions prevail on both sides of the problem. Many church members in the South are employed in textiles; as workers, managers, or owners. The issues are part of a human-rights context. They focus on the right of workers to organize, the obligation of management to bargain in "good faith," the use of power by those in control, the right to a just and equitable wage and to safe and healthful working conditions, and the "right to work." The ultimate concern is not only economic justice but human dignity and the right of people to participate in decision about their life and work.

How Southern churches and their pastors will handle the growing pressures is a continuing question. There is doubt that the controversy will be resolved quickly or easily. At the same time there is growing realization, not only at the national level, but at the regional and local levels that the church has a responsibility to address itself to justice concerns in labor-management relationships. In this regard the regional and local church can and should provide resources and guidelines for ethical decision making and the enhancement of human dignity. Social, political, and economic rights are part of that process.   F.L.J.

Hubert H. Humphrey and Martin Luther King, Jr.

Any discussion of both the intellectual concept and the practical implementation of "human rights" opens up the dangers of overstating the case or underestimating the problem. The church can generalize human rights so that it becomes broad and bland. Another possibility is to emphasize one note or idea to the exclusion of other matters of equality.

The opening article by Dr. George Brand helps us to see the dangers. We can denounce Russia and its oppression of rights; we could also fail to speak because the U.S. record is clouded— especially in the history of civil rights. The biblical article likewise gives us excellent guidance. Preachers and teachers can turn every biblical text into an activist harangue; we could also remain silent on rights issues as we talk of evangelism or fund-raising campaigns.

With that understanding, let us approach the issue from the specific history and experience of two individuals. Early in 1978, January 15, to be exact, several people—including this writer— walked past a flag-draped casket in the rotunda of our nation's Capitol. There lay the body of an exponent and practicer of human rights in America, Hubert H. Humphrey. Truly his death left many Americans saddened. We are saddened because there are simply not many individuals who, like Humphrey, live as constantly and effectively what they believe about equal rights. His place in the U.S. Senate and as vice-president of our nation gave him an opportunity to personalize civil liberty and to work domestically for the rights of all people. Bless him, he did it!

Thirty years earlier, Humphrey challenged the Democratic Party and the American people to "get out of the shadows of states rights into the glorious sunshine of human rights." Late in 1977, in his last speech in the halls of Congress, he said that democracy is "an endangered species." He told all of us that "we must be strong for freedom and justice . . . We must be strong for opportunity, for *equal* opportunity." It might seem strange to use a Washington politician as an example of the way to decide how to work for human rights. Humphrey introduced human-rights legislation before most people were ready, and continued to press for action while many debated theology and methodology. Caution and moderation cloaked a lack of conviction and courage to *do* human rights.

On that same day, in the city of Atlanta, Georgia, memorial services were held in Ebenezer Baptist Church led by Martin

Luther King, Sr. Many words of tribute were spoken about Martin Luther King, Jr., who would have been 49 years of age on that day. And equal words of praise were spoken also about Hubert H. Humphrey. As Martin Luther King, Sr. spoke that day, it was clear that his life is literally dedicated to continue the nonviolent human-rights effort of his son.

The point is that human rights can be reality as well as rhetoric. Humphrey and King were great vocal exponents of freedom and justice. More important, their lives were an expression and claim for human rights for all people. Thus those who preach the word in pulpits, as King so often did, do not always need specific texts, verses, or passages to speak of human rights. God has made obvious to us that all of life is for all people. This is to be true in the church and it is to be true in all of God's world. From creation to the resurrection of our Lord and the early days of the church, God has prodded his people to speak for equal rights and to take up the cross for those who are not granted equality.

The politician Humphrey and the preacher King met often. They took the challenge of freedom and justice—of human rights—to the people. They put flesh and bones on the rhetoric of human rights.

Surely in Washington, D.C., in Ottawa, Canada, and in all the capitals of the world, human rights can be talked about and legislation enacted. George Brand reminds us that even in countries under Communist governments there are those speaking and working for human rights. The United States is not the sole custodian or dispenser of rights. Yet we are challenged to use our gifts and freedom of expression. God's love and care for people is truly unleashed in the world.

Many examples of the House of Representatives' and the Senate's involvement in human rights can be identified. The 95th Congress has labored over an energy bill. It has concerned itself about the criminal code, native Americans, refugees, and strip mining. The broad areas of welfare and health care touch the reality of the rights of people, especially the poor.

South Africa, Namibia, and other parts of the world have been in the news month after month. The conference in Belgrade sought to implement the work of the United Nations and of people working for the rights of all. Certainly pastors must proclaim justice and rights for all people. As elections take place this year, Christians should listen carefully to what candidates say they will do in the field of human rights.

Let us be more specific about the opportunities for members of our churches. The IMPACT network gives individuals across the country an opportunity for joining in issues of rights. Laity and clergy can join IMPACT (110 Maryland Avenue, N.E. Washington, D.C. 20002). There is a task force within IMPACT on civil rights and civil liberties.

Pastors and leaders could do much in encouraging members of congregations to visit state or provincial capitals and their nation's capital to see what really happens in God's world of politics and human rights. There are some new Hubert Humphreys and Martin Lurther Kings still alive in the world and in the church. All that some of our Christian leaders need is a real vision and experience of what can be done. It will demand more than quoting Matthew, Romans, and Amos. It will include conviction and courage so that they can challenge others to work for the rights of those completely separated from the church. God is the ultimate deterrent to inhuman treatment.   C. V. B.

African Polygamy and Christian Mission

What image of Christianity are we projecting in those societies which traditionally regard polygamy or plural marriage as a preferential form of marriage? This is a serious question today among the churches in Africa where the gospel is presented to peoples for whom polygamy is a socially approved, honored, and preferential system with deep cultural roots.

Involved is the credibility of the church's evangelizing mission. It is also a serious pastoral problem. Most of the churches have fairly consistently, and sometimes very persistently, opposed polygamy.

Western Christians have commonly considered monogamy to be the best expression of marriage. But this concept of marriage has produced serious problems for the church in the nonwestern world. This is especially true in those situations where it is demanded, as a condition for baptism, that a polygamist of another culture should divorce one or more of his wives. Such an insistence on monogamy has worked against the stability of marriage, against the concept of fidelity, and against the most vital ties established between families and clans.

Questions are increasingly raised: Should the proclamation of the gospel threaten human rights and family stability, disrupt social relations, and separate mothers from their children? Is it possible for the church to permit the baptism of a polygamist and his wives, if the gospel has reached them in this situation?

Plural marriage, or polygamy, is found throughout the world in a variety of forms that are culturally determined. The familiar form among Western peoples is *consecutive* polygamy: one spouse after another in sequence involving divorce and remarriage. Elsewhere in the world plural marriage usually means *simultaneous* polygamy: more than one spouse at the same time. In Africa it is a culturally determined, socially acceptable, and legally recognized form of permanent marriage. Polygamy is also a widely recognized and socially valid form of marriage in parts of New Guinea, Papua, Indonesia, and in most of the Islamic world.

There is no suggestion that polygamy should be introduced into the Western world. Church members of all confessional groups in Africa today ask whether the marriage institution as understood and held to in the Western world belongs particularly to that culture and has not taken seriously the conception and realities of marriage elsewhere. Study is being carried out in all churches with respect to the authenticity, validity, and correctness of the various answers previously given by the Christian churches to the perplexing questions raised by plural marriage in Africa.

One Methodist bishop, in light of his experiences in Angola and southeastern Africa, asks the following questions: How can we respond to this problem in ways that promote human rights, love, and justice? Is monogamy a prior condition for baptism? Is acceptance of the law of monagamy to be identified with faith in Jesus Christ, and is it to be a condition *sine qua non* for admission into the Christian fellowship? What is our responsibility for those wives who are divorced by a husband with plural wives who desire to be baptized? How have we compromised their previously contracted rights, their social status, economic security, and even their relationships with their children? Is it more just to have polygamy than organized prostitution, marital infidelity with impunity, a rapidly growing divorce rate, and increasing numbers of illegitimate children? Is it more wholesome for young women to become prostitutes, call girls, or mistresses than to become the second or third wives of a respected member of the community? Is permitting youth to choose their own mates necessarily more moral than an agreement among families?

Bishop Josiah Kibira of the Evangelical Lutheran Church in Tanzania has stated that the greatest ethical problems for the church are divorce and polygamy and the question of church discipline. And of these questions, the problem of polygamy is the most difficult. Perhaps, he states, we may find by theological study that we should not prevent a pagan polygamist from being baptized if he is called while in that condition.

For Bishop Peter Sarpong of the Roman Catholic Church in Kenya, the widespread African custom of polygamy is also a pressing pastoral problem. The majority of the bishops agree that there is a need for more research and education, and even a rethinking of the traditional response to the question of polygamy. The Roman Catholic position has been relatively clear. To be baptized a polygamist may retain only one wife, the first wife of the plural marriage, since the greatest claim to validity belonged to the first marriage.

In general the various Protestant solutions to the problem of polygamy may be summarized as follows: When the members of a polygamous family have been called to the new life of Christian faith (1) all the women and children may be baptized, but not the husband, (2) only those who are not polygamously married may be baptized, (3) the husband may be baptized, if he divorces all but the preferred wife, (4) all may be baptized with the understanding that any subsequent plural marriages are forbidden, (5) on the testimony of their faith alone, any of them may be baptized with no previous conditions. The variety of approaches and the general lack of consistency among the churches has only added to the problem.

The Bremen Mission early maintained a pastoral policy in these words: "Polygamy existed at the time of Christ and the apostles, but we do not find that monogamy was made a condition for acceptance into the church. Therefore, a man who has several wives must be admitted to baptism and communion; however, all are always to be reminded that monogamy is the true married state according to God, and that only in this way can the purpose of marriage be reached."

The Lutheran Church in Liberia decided in 1951 that polygamous husbands as well as their wives may be admitted to baptism and communion, although normally they may not hold official positions of leadership in the ecclesiastical organization.

The few churches presently following the admission to baptism and communion of members of a polygamous family firmly uphold the ideal of monogamy, but have come to recognize that the rejection of polygamy does not always demand the rejection of men who were polygamists before the Christian message was presented to them. Unfortunately, the response to this question is not always consistent, even within the same church. West African Anglicans, for example, do allow the wives of polygamists to be baptized, but in South Africa and elsewhere they are not even admitted to the catechumenate without the authorization of the bishop in each case.

In general it is the independent African churches, often composed initially of dissident Christians from churches which grew as a result of Western missionary efforts, which have taken the most lenient positions. While some of these churches have repudiated polygamy, others have merely upheld monogamy more as an ideal than as a normal practice. Some have positively accepted polygamy as a part of their conscious indigenization of Christianity in Africa. As a result some have been excluded from ecumenical fellowship and have not been regarded as authentic Christian communities. The law of monogamy becomes therefore a criterion of Christian faith and a mark of the true church.

The questions keep pressing and changes of attitude and practice come also. A helpful review of the problems of polygamy in Africa is found in Eugene Hillman, *Polygamy Reconsidered* (Maryknoll, N.Y.: Orbis, 1975).   R. C. W.

CHRIST AND POWER
by Martin Hengel, Everett R. Kalin trans.; Fortress, 1977; 96 pages; $3.25

The conflict of Christ and his church with the world's political powers is the theme of this biblical and historical survey by a professor of New Testament at the University of Tübingen.

Jesus' unique power was displayed as he proclaimed God's lordship over humanity. The power of Christ was the power of God's forgiving and serving love. New life was given through his authoritative word and helping deeds. He exercised only charismatic authority while inaugurating God's kingdom and battling against the ruling powers of his day.

While Jesus appeared socially dangerous to the apathetic Sadducees, he was probably viewed as politically reactionary by the revolutionary Zealots. Though he died on the cross as a political criminal, his disarming power lay not least in his renunciation of external force while exercising the compelling power of the Holy Spirit.

Hengel sketches the problems raised by this evangelical stance during the persecutions of the early church and the compromises of the imperial church. He evaluates Augustine's vision of the Two Cities and Luther's doctrine of the Two Kingdoms as creative though imperfect restatements of Paul's teaching of the Two Ages in Adam and Christ. All intend to witness to the eschatological uniqueness of God's inbreaking kingdom in protest against all attempts to intermingle political power and spiritual authority in a theocratic state governed by a "theology of glory."

In the current German debate Hengel attacks both Lutheran quietists and Reformed activists as betraying the authority of Christ. He rejects the "restoration theology" of those Lutheran conservatives who blindly endorse nationalism, capitalism, nuclear weapons, and capital punishment. He also criticizes the "political theology" of those Barthian radicals who uncritically identify the church with socialism, armed revolution in the Third World, and the Marxist one-part system.

Hengel's mutual corrective is the biblical affirmation that the lordship of Christ extends into the secular realm through the just and loving service of involved Christians and churches. W. H. L.

SOCIAL PHILOSOPHY
by Joel Feinberg; Prentice-Hall, 1973; 125 pages; $4.95

Here is a welcome head clearer for sufferers of rhetorical overload. Published in 1973 before human rights was politically "in," this short paperback sets forth a useful methodology and framework for thinking about freedom, social justice, and rights.

Feinberg makes no bold claims for independently existing rights which are either "self-evident" to reason or revealed to faith. Principles, he contends, are to be stated tentatively and then tested in borderline situations involving conflict with other principles of corresponding weight. The task of achieving a "reflective equilibrium" among moral claims is an ongoing one.

The author's helpful differentiation between human rights and legal rights stands as a critique of the tendencies either to couch human rights in specific legal language or to attempt the legislation of moral ideals. In discussing "universality" and "nonconflictability," Feinberg concludes that, except for the right not to be tortured, there are probably no rights that are in any sense absolute and without qualification.

Christians will not agree with Feinberg's assertion (p.94) that human worth or dignity "is not grounded on anything more ultimate than itself"; yet they will not quarrel with the author's statement immediately following that such basic worth "is not demonstrably justifiable." It is clearly a matter of faith, whatever the name of one's ultimate concern. There is nothing "self-evident" or "self-revealing" in it, the Declaration of Independence to the contrary notwithstanding.

The political task of converting principle into policy is driven by will and power. Yet, it requires the operation of the intellect as well. Feinberg has made a valuable contribution to the pursuit of justice based upon sound moral reflection.   R. J. N.

FROM UNDER THE RUBBLE
by Alexander Solzhenitsyn, et al; Little, Brown and Company, 1975; 308 pages; $8.95

The six authors of these eleven essays have all clashed in one way or another with the Soviet government. The publication of this book in Paris (in Russian) and in the U.S.A. (in English) is an in-dication of the status of the right to free speech in the Soviet Union. But the essays deal with a broad spectrum of human rights, with implications for countries outside the U.S.S.R.

The theme which runs through the essays is the necessity of the transformation of public life through ethics and moral and spiritual means, rather than only through regular politics. Readers may disagree with this apparently sharp separation. However, several of the essays make a forceful argument that only such a transformation can break the inertia and repression of "business as usual" in politics and government, whether in the U.S.S.R. or Western nations.

The essays on socialism and alternatives to it pose challenges to the economic aspects of human rights for capitalist systems as well. Two essays on the status of the Orthodox Church in the U.S.S.R. ask questions about the church in the world which are equally pertinent to North America. The essays on ethnic and radical groups within the Soviet Union speak also to the problems of human rights and racism in our culture.

For North American readers the extensive discussion of the history which has led to the current situation in the U.S.S.R. may be an alien perspective—given our tendency to be more future- than past-oriented. However, only by taking seriously our roots can we address the other major theme of the book: what should be the role of the nation within international political life of the future? The perspective of these Soviet dissidents should help us to ask new and pertinent questions about our new understanding of human rights.   E. A. B.

THE VAST MAJORITY: A JOURNEY TO THE WORLD'S POOR
by Michael Harrington; Simon & Schuster, 1977; 281 pages; $9.95

Combining technical scholarship with personal reflections based on travels in Asia, Africa, and Latin America Harrington presents a shattering indictment of the current international economic arrangements that are dominated by the rich nations. His analysis demonstrates that U.S. trade policy, the nature of U.S. foreign investments and foreign aid, as well as the monetary policies of the International Monetary Fund (IMF) and the World Bank, result in the continued dependence of the poor countries on the rich countries. In other words, there is a vested interest to develop underdevelopment.

Harrington argues persuasively that this division of the world into rich and poor is not the consequence of some inevitable law of nature. Rather, it is the result of an international economic order specifically designed to transfer resources from the desperate to the privileged.

The high-protein flour that is produced in Peru is not consumed by a hungry population. It is exported to Europe and the United States where it is fed to livestock. In Central America and the Caribbean the best half of the agricultural land grows crops for export while 70 percent of the children suffer from malnutrition. In Haiti the peasants go hungry while the cultivated land is utilized for low nutrition and feed crops for export.

The terms of international trade have systematically favored the affluent over the impoverished. As a result there has been a steady outflow of profits and fees from the backward to the advanced economies. This constant drain of capital has forced the lesser developed countries to borrow to such an extent that their current debt is approximately $200 billion. Many of these countries can hardly pay the interest rates before they are compelled to apply for new loans. They exist in a state of permanent bondage.

Harrington makes an impassioned plea for a new international economic order.   G. H. B.

The Rights of the Weak

As has been pointed out so clearly, the notion of "human rights" is not very prominent in the Bible or for that matter in the classic Christian faith. Here the emphasis is on obligations, to God, to the neighbor, and to ourselves—even to our body, which should be a temple of the Holy Spirit.

Nevertheless, the Bible does speak occasionally of human rights. Isaiah exclaims: "Woe to those who decree iniquitous decrees, and the writers who keep writing oppression to turn aside the needy from justice and to rob the poor of my people of their *right (mishpat)*, that widows may be their spoil and that they may make the fatherless their prey!" (Isa. 10:1–2). Similar expressions are found in Jeremiah 6:26–28, and Lamentation 3:34–36 asserts that the Lord does not approve when the "right of man" is turned aside.

Even if "human rights" as we use the term today is a child of the Enlightenment, the peculiar way in which it is juxtaposed with the Creator in the American tradition is not without significance for Christians. If the notion of "human rights" is ever to contribute to justice, this connection must be made more explicit.

It may have been an afterthought in the mind of Thomas Jefferson to assert that the *Creator* endowed human beings with certain inalienable rights. He may, indeed, have been more interested in the rights of white, male Virginians than in those of blacks or women. He may have thrown in the Creator as a sop to the pious. But as we have lived with these notions for more than two hundred years, it has become ever more apparent that without grounding these rights in something else than some transient political ideology, the will of the majority or some "scientific" anthropology—or even the interpretations of the Supreme Court, they will be fleeting indeed.

The majority giveth and the majority taketh away. Anybody who has ever confronted the power of *eminent domain* ("that superior dominion of the sovereign power over property within the state which authorizes it to appropriate all or any part thereof to a necessary public use, reasonable compensation being made,") or even the IRS, could tell eloquent tales. And what happens if "scientific" anthropology demonstrates that some races are more intelligent than others? Or that some human beings are by its "scientific" definition not human at all? All people are equal, but some are obviously more equal than others.

And the courts? The present Supreme Court of the United States, with its consistent denial of equal rights to the powerless—e.g. the right of life of the fetus versus the right of privacy of the mother, or the logically similar decision that since abortion is a private matter it should be paid for privately—does not appear to be a strong bulwark behind which the poor, the widows, the fatherless, the needy can find refuge.

Where do we stand in the present clamor about rights? Men and women, black and white, East and West, North and South, old and young, drivers and pedestrians, tenants and landlords—the list of claimants is endless.

A sound rule of thumb for Christians in this vast controversy may be found in Isaiah and Jeremiah. They always talk about the rights of the weak. We have an obligation to defend the weak against the strong—precisely because the strong are able to take care of themselves. And if one group which once was very strong should happen to become weak—we might have to shift sides. We may agree here with Emerson who said: "A foolish consistency is the hobgoblin of little minds adored by little statesmen and philosophers and divines."

As the Parable of the Good Samaritan teaches, we are called to defend the human rights of those who, because they are weak and have fallen among robbers, need our help most. But as the parable also teaches, human beings are our concern—not abstract causes.

It does not mean that we ought to defend monarchy—since

kings have fallen on evil days. But we might defend the right to a fair trial for a king who has lost his kingdom. The rights of terrorists do not deserve defense, the rights of terrorists who have been caught do. To gloat when "evil people" are crushed by "good people" is a very normal human reaction. This made the motion picture *Star Wars* such a success. It usually means, however, that "their" people are crushed by "our" people. The unusual feature of the action of the Good Samaritan was that he helped one of "theirs," merely because the man who was robbed was in desperate need.

That is why Jesus used the Good Samaritan as an example of what it means to be a neighbor and to respect the rights of somebody in need. For this reason he can also serve as an example in our present discussion of human rights. In the complicated and confusing debate about human rights we are to defend the rights of the weak against the strong. Who they are at any one time will depend on the situation. Isaiah and Jeremiah have given us a helpful clue.   G. W. F.